CULTURE
SHIFT

*The
Employee Handbook
for Changing
Corporate Culture*

PRICE PRITCHETT, P.H.D.

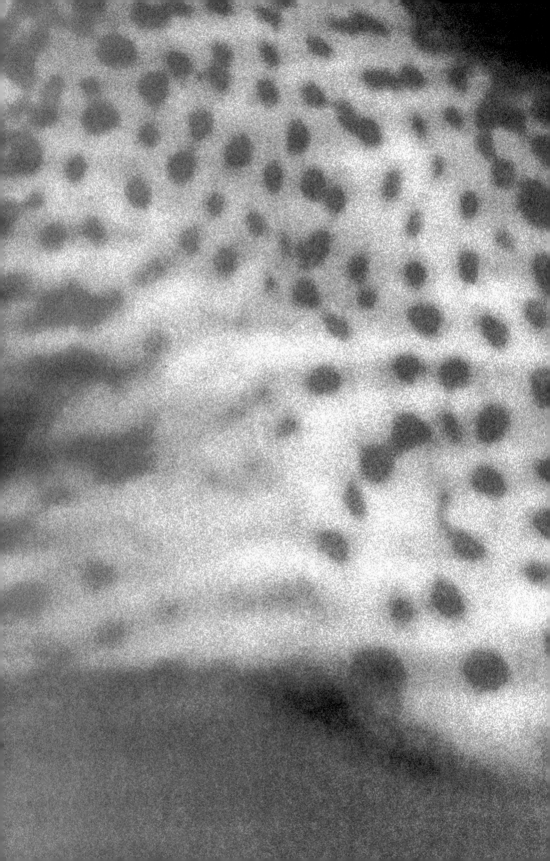

Y ou are an architect of the corporate culture. You shape it by how you behave. Every single thing you do serves as one more building block in the habit patterns that make up the personality – the culture – of the company.

In time the culture takes on a life of its own. It gains power and influence. And as the habits grow stronger, the culture begins to shape *your* behavior more and more.

Culture can be very controlling. But powerful as it might be, the culture cannot change without permission from the people.

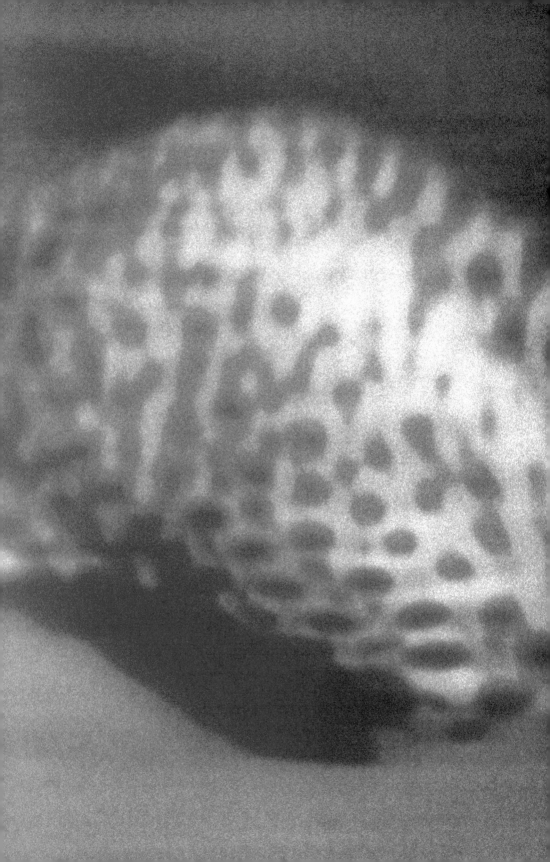

The problems come when the world changes but the culture can't...because people in the organization won't give it a chance.

Today – in our world of high-velocity change – the culture needs your help in order to break its bad habits. You need to teach it better ways to behave. It relies on you to give it a new set of responses that hold more promise for the future.

CC Mal.

17 — play it sye
29 — be loyal to the culture
27 — protect yaself.

PRITCHETT & ASSOCIATES, INC.
Dallas, Texas

Table of Contents

Choose a sheet and apply a behavior ie

Fast History

Something you may be able to have an impact on.

Fast History

Change keeps picking up speed. Before the organization can finish getting adjusted to one change, it gets hit with several others. We're living in a constant period of transition, and the shelf life of our solutions keeps getting shorter. "What works" becomes history in a hurry.

Where is all this change coming from? Well, to begin with, *people* create change. So let's look at what's happening to the head count on Mother Earth.

Human beings have been around for some six or seven million years. It took that long for the population of the earth to reach 5.3 billion people. But the predictions say that it will take only about 50 years for the *next* 5.3 billion people to be here. If people create change – and obviously they do – then we should expect a rapid *increase* in the rate of change as the population doubles in the next few decades.

This growing crowd of people is armed with another source of change: Technology. And technology feeds on itself. So let's review what's happening in the area of science, inventions, and technology in general.

Word has it that more than 80% of our technological inventions have occurred just since 1900. Also, it is predicted that within the last 15 years of the twentieth century we will see as much technological change as there was in the first 85 years. Don't think of technological change as something that keeps merely adding up – think of it as *multiplying* on a daily basis.

Still another source of change is knowledge. Information. According to the book, *Information Anxiety*, the fund of information available to us doubles every five years.

More people, more tools, more knowledge. And here's the bottom line: Maybe you think you've seen a lot of change lately, but you haven't seen anything yet. The future promises us more change than we've ever experienced before, and it will come at us faster and faster. The question is, will we give our *culture* permission to change such that the organization can survive in a world of fast history?

Change has no conscience. Doesn't play favorites. Takes no prisoners. And change ruthlessly destroys organizations with cultures that don't adapt. Just look around – it's happening to companies everywhere.

In years past we could get by with a slower response time. Change didn't move as fast back then. Competition wasn't as stiff. Also, the world gave us more room for recovery. There was enough space between major change events for people to catch their breath and collect their senses. Many of the "normal" human reactions to the stress of change worked okay. Our old culture could cope. But those days belong in the history books now.

A world of high-velocity change calls for radical shifts in behavior. Specifically, we must think differently. Reorder our priorities. Develop faster reflexes. Give the culture an entirely new set of responses.

We can't afford to ignore change and just do what comes naturally. We must face reality and do what *works*.

"There's no off-season anymore."

Nolan Ryan,

Texas Rangers' pitcher and world record holder for no-hitters,

in commercial for Advil

Slow Down. Speed Up.

When change hits, a common response is caution. Faced with the unfamiliar, surrounded by uncertainty, the organization gears down. On the surface it makes sense. You really can't do much to reduce the speed of change. But if *you* slow down, you somehow feel a little safer. So people put on the brakes, hoping to buy some time.

But change won't wait on you. You simply don't have time to take your time.

"Carefulness" actually gets dangerous when it creates a culture of caution – paralysis sets in, the organization loses momentum, and problems start to multiply. Under today's conditions, slowing down is the most hazardous move you could make.

Hurry needs to become the normal style, and merely picking up the pace a little won't work. Competition moves so fast. Markets change so quickly. Technology advances at a dead run. The world wants instant everything. The result? Good goes bad in a hurry. And the level of performance that qualifies you as a winner today can make you a has-been tomorrow.

Do everything possible to accelerate, to create a culture with quicker reflexes. Hustle. Put speed and responsiveness into every aspect of the business. Help get rid of bureaucratic practices and "busy work" that bog down productivity. Break down the boundaries between work groups, so communication flows fast and freely. Understand that the organization can't afford to carry any extra weight, and that downsizing and de-layering may be needed to create a leaner, fleeter, more agile outfit. Don't resist change, because that's a drag on the organization. The culture counts on you to give it a sense of urgency.

Slowing down gives you the feeling that you're safer, more in control. But the feeling is false. Picking up speed protects you better in today's world of high-velocity change.

"Time used to be a tyrant. Today it's an assassin."

From an R.R. Donnelley & Sons
Company advertisement

~~Panic.~~ Stay Cool.

Change scares a lot of people. Facing the unknown gets spooky. Even knowing what's coming can rattle your nerves. A sense of helplessness can hit if you get the idea that you have no control over your destiny. Sometimes these feelings get so intense they produce a culture of panic.

When fear leads to frenzy, the result is lousy judgment, poorly conceived plans, and too much wasted motion. Panic kills your concentration, causes you to jump to conclusions, and leads to reckless behavior – all this at the very time when the organization needs you to be at your best.

When change shakes the organization, you need to hold steady. A levelheaded way of looking at the situation keeps you from going off half-cocked. Action is important, but acting impulsively will probably only make things worse.

Change *should* get your attention. It should give you an emotional charge, and you should take it seriously. The secret is knowing how to scramble without getting spastic, how to be more intense and still in control.

Use the energy that change generates to give the culture a greater sense of urgency. But stay focused. Rather than bouncing around like a pinball, haphazardly ricocheting from one worry to the next, find out what counts the most. Stick with that. Frantic activity keeps you busy – leaving you emotionally drained, and eventually burned out – without much of true importance being accomplished.

Success under these conditions comes from cool-headed thinking, clear focus, and well aimed action. Help create a culture that is steady under fire.

"Sometimes I think the world has gone completely mad.
And then I think, 'Aw, who cares?'
And then I think, 'Hey, what's for supper?'"

Jack Handey,

"Deep Thoughts" from Saturday Night Live

Wait for Instructions.

Take the
Initiative.

Change can easily create a culture of dependence. Maybe you feel uncertain, or confused, so you decide to sit back until you get a new set of directions. You've got questions that need answers. You want help.

It could be that you're disgusted. Let's say you don't buy in to the changes, so you figure you'll hold off until somebody comes around and tells you specifically what to do. After all, "doing nothing" is one of the popular ways people fight changes they don't like.

Of course, it might be that the culture hasn't required you to think for yourself. Maybe you assume you're *supposed* to wait for guidance, to always turn to your boss for assignments, so you've just naturally come to depend on others for your marching orders.

Those days are over. The shift toward a culture of initiative and independence means you must figure out for yourself what the organization needs. Then move on it.

Self-directed behavior is essential in today's world of accelerating change. For one thing, organizations are learning to run lean, and that means every person must become more self-sufficient. You can't count on having someone to come around and hand-feed you instructions on a regular basis.

Besides, higher management may not be in a position to help much. Often the boss doesn't get to see problems as quickly as you do. Or doesn't understand how to fix them as well as you do. Plus, the boss usually isn't there when the opportunity to improve things pops up.

So put yourself in charge of problem-solving. You don't have to have all the answers. Nobody does. Just show some initiative. Come up with your own answers, and there's a good chance they'll be better than you could get from anybody else.

You slow down the organization when you go looking for help…when you depend on someone else to tell you what to do…or when you wage a sneaky war against change by waiting for instructions. Show some initiative, and you'll see the organization start picking up speed.

"If you come to a fork in the road, take it."

Attributed to Yogi Berra

Get Ready.

Rapid change calls for a rapid response, but people often bog down in planning *how* to react. They confuse getting ready with actual progress. They diddle away precious time *preparing* to do something.

You can analyze the situation to death: Weigh the facts…consider your options…get organized…calculate the best plan of attack…then take forever to debug that plan.

Meanwhile, the beat goes on. Change, and the problems it creates, won't wait on you to come up with a foolproof approach. Trouble is a moving target, giving you little time to take aim. By the time you come up with a perfect plan, the problems will have moved on you. And probably grown bigger. Getting ready gets dangerous when it creates a culture of delay.

You can take time to roll up your sleeves, but that's about it. Today's rapid rate of change calls for a culture of mobility. Put your faith in action rather than analysis, in pursuit instead of painstaking preparation.

Your job is to help the organization dramatically shrink the time it takes to get things done. This means you must be willing to improvise, to feel your way along. You can't afford to stop and study the situation from all angles before you make a move. Instead of trying to analyze and plan your way through problems, *learn* your way through the situation.

Inertia is more crippling than mistakes. Inaction is the most costly error. So just get going. Mobility will be your best teacher. It's the fastest way to find out what works and what doesn't.

Just keep moving. When you foul up, fix it. Learn from your mistakes, and plow on. This is how you energize the organization and build momentum. Create a culture of action that can keep up in a world of constant change.

. "No plan survives contact with the enemy."

Field Marshal Helmuth Carl Bernard von Moltke

Try Harder. Try Easier.

People commonly respond to the stress of change by putting out more effort. The greater the change (that is, the bigger the adjustment they need to make) the harder they try. But they stick with the same old habits. They bet the future on "more of the same." Their heart is in the right place, their intentions are good, but they fail to realize that many solutions of the past don't fit the problems of the future. In fact, a lot of today's problems are actually *caused* by yesterday's solutions.

You can't handle change very well if *you* don't change – no matter how determined you are, and regardless of how hard you try. Really, now, how much faster or better can you do things if you basically keep doing them the same old way? Just how much more effort is it *possible* to give? Sooner or later you reach your limit. Trying harder – while using the same old tools, techniques, and thinking patterns – creates a culture of desperation.

The secret is to simplify. Search for different solutions. Easier ones.

Look for shortcuts, ways to save time and money and effort without sacrificing high standards. Eliminate unnecessary steps. Ask, "Why are we doing that?" Get rid of things that get in the way. Find a better approach.

Innovate. Bust out of your old routines. Be willing to make a radical change. If the organization expects you to do more with less, to do it better and quicker, your only hope is to find an easier approach.

Try easier. Build a culture that believes in simplicity.

"The less effort, the faster and more powerful you will be."

Bruce Lee,

expert in martial arts

~~Waste Time and Energy on Emotions.~~

Spend
Energy
on
Solutions.

Sometimes change creates a culture of complaint. People get mad at the situation. They gripe. They burn up precious energy on frustration and angry feelings. Some play "poor me," whine about being a victim, and dwell on what they've lost. They wallow around in wishful thinking, and long for a return of the "good old days." Still others waste themselves on worry – about the future, what they might lose, or what all could go wrong.

None of this negative thinking improves a thing.

Change makes a lot of new demands on people, leaving you little time or energy to spare. So instead of getting upset and wasting these precious resources, spend them on solving the new problems.

Buckle down. Channel your thoughts and efforts along productive lines. Get busy instead of getting mad. Crowd out unpleasant emotions by filling your mind with a search for solutions.

Action is better therapy than tears. And doing your part to help the organization adjust will lower your level of emotional stress a lot better than resisting the changes ever would.

Redirect grief, anger, or worry into a passionate pursuit of results. Work from the heart, and you heal the spirit. Put fire into your job habits, and you burn off worry and anger.

Spend your energy and time on finding solutions to the problems of change. You can help shape the culture into an energy-efficient system.

"When you win, nothing hurts."

Joe Namath,

Hall of Fame quarterback

Play it
Safe.

Take
More Risks.

Change redefines where the biggest gambles lie. No longer is there safety in the status quo, in trying to conduct business as usual, or in sticking with what brought success in the past. The so-called conservative approach has become the biggest crapshoot of all.

The surest security in today's world comes from a willingness to take risks. You need *nerve*.

Guts give the best odds for success because the organization's future depends on its ability to find better ways to do business. A culture unwilling to experiment has little chance to innovate. It gets stuck in its own history. Without the courage to risk, it can't expect to crack the code for breakthroughs.

Unless employees give themselves permission to be pioneers – to explore, to go forward without guarantees, to move toward the future without road maps – the organization will always trail behind the competition. In this fiercely competitive world of ours, that's *not* playing it safe. That's taking reckless chances which threaten the organization's very survival.

You need to use your imagination. Try out some wild ideas. Break out of those old routines and do something different. Extend yourself – see how far you can reach. Put some adventure into your approach instead of handling work in the common, conventional manner.

Doing things the same old way may seem a lot safer, but it actually hurts the organization's chances for success. A culture where people won't stick their necks out won't find it easy to win.

"Make a bet every day, otherwise you might walk around lucky and never know it."

Jimmy Jones

~~*Rely More Heavily on Your Strengths.*~~

Don't Let Strengths Become Weaknesses.

P ut people under pressure – like the stress that comes from dealing with
change – and they usually turn to their strengths. It's human nature, and on
the surface it makes sense: Rely on what you do best…fight with your
favorite weapons…stick with well developed habits where you really shine.

But what if conditions call for new moves? What if doing what you do best
quits working very well?

When people are doing the wrong things – even if they do them flawlessly –
the organization has trouble coping. Strengths become weaknesses when circumstances change but behavior doesn't.

A culture of inflexibility develops if people put too much faith in their
strengths. So be prepared to abandon your best moves. Show respect for
what *works*. Go ahead and give the organization what it needs most – even if
it's not your strong suit. Be willing to stumble along. You can get better
you go. If you're doing the right things, you don't have to do them perfectly
get great results.

The key is to keep learning. Develop in new directions. Adapt. Don't get
ed in to a set of skills or an approach that could become outdated. Be willing
nd, to adjust, because a rapidly changing world requires new competencies.
our part to keep the culture from getting stiff.

"There is no permanent solution."

Price Pritchett

~~Try Not to Break Things.~~

Welcome Destruction.

Change, by its very nature, is destructive. It gets messy. It causes confusion. That bothers a lot of people. They warn against change, or argue for taking it slow and easy so nothing gets broken. If they get their way, the organization has to tiptoe around, try to be neat, and not hurt anybody or upset people. Eventually, such a culture gets the organization in big trouble.

A culture that's unwilling to break things can't move fast. If it tries to salvage everything, it ends up carrying a lot of old baggage. Bureaucratic practices and all kinds of other bad habits build up over time. Even beloved tradition can anchor the organization to its past, making it tough to respond to the pull of the future. Protecting what "is" often sabotages what "could be."

It may sound strange, but destruction is one of today's conditions for survival. Just as a snake sheds a skin it has outgrown, the culture needs to rid itself of habits that have outlived their usefulness.

Help do away with bureaucratic practices that get in the way. Break with tradition when it becomes an obstacle. Don't be afraid to butcher the sacred cows. Instead of blindly protecting old beliefs, throw them against the rocks of reality to see if they bounce or shatter. Be willing to smash some glass.

Sure, all this gets messy. It makes a lot of noise. Some people will get upset. But organizations – and individuals – always must make certain sacrifices if they want to stay strong.

Help create a culture where people are rewarded for disturbing the peace.

"If evolution was worth its salt, by now it should've evolved
something better than survival of the fittest."

Jane Wagner

~~*Avoid Mistakes.*~~

Make More
Mistakes.

Change often leaves people feeling exposed…vulnerable…insecure. They get jumpy about doing anything that might make them look bad. Fear of foul-ups causes them to freeze up. Productivity nosedives. It's a common problem when the organization makes it safer to do nothing rather than do wrong.

Cultures that don't tolerate failure also have trouble developing new competencies. People can't afford to experiment. They have to stick with what they know. And fixing problems gets tough when folks are reluctant to use trial-and-error to find out what works.

Fear of mistakes locks learning out of your work. It limits your repertoire. Failure, on the other hand, is the master educator. Rapid innovation, in particular, almost always grows out of a high error rate: More attempts, quicker insight, faster solutions.

Obviously, this does not give you a license to get careless or do dumb things. Sloppy, halfhearted effort can never benefit the culture. Honest mistakes, though, are life's main schoolroom. Usually success is a direct byproduct of screw-ups.

On the surface it sounds irresponsible, but to flourish in a rapidly changing world you actually need to make more mistakes. Fail quickly. Fail often. If you do something and it doesn't work, just recover in a hurry and try something else.

Look at your job as a laboratory. Try things. Experiment. Know going in that many of the things you attempt won't pan out, but that those mistakes can still light the way to success. Help develop a culture that is willing to fail its way to the future.

"You miss 100% of the shots you never take."

Wayne Gretsky,
hockey star

23

~~Shave~~
~~Standards.~~

Shoot for
Total Quality.

Change has a way of bringing out the best, the worst, and the so-so in people. The "iffy" behavior, this so-so stuff, occurs when people make a habit out of shaving standards in their efforts to cope.

Pressed to keep up with change – to do more with less – some people play fast *and loose*. They shrug off the idea of excellence in an effort to pick up a little speed. Scrambling to cover the necessary ground, they make sacrifices in the quality of their performance.

The slippage begins when employees cut themselves some slack. They excuse themselves for giving less than their best and create a culture of mediocrity. Considering the circumstances – the pressure, the stress, all the new demands – they rationalize that it's okay to go the quick-and-dirty route...to settle for lower quality work...or to relax on issues relating to ethics and integrity. Maybe there's even a little revenge at work here sometimes. For example, shaving standards is a way of getting even with the organization when you don't like what's going on.

Shaving standards doesn't look like a major violation. But when enough people get lax in the chase to get things done, the organization's reputation gets a little shabby. Customers start to drift toward the competition. Naturally, this puts the organization at even greater risk.

Raise your standards, and pursue a culture of total quality. Make no compromises – in your personal ethics, the calibre of your output, or your overall productivity. Instead of accepting less than your best, *improve* on it. Reach for new and higher benchmarks. Stay on the highroad in your ethical standards.

Don't tolerate so-so performance, in yourself or anybody else. Now, during the tough times, is when you really define the character of the culture.

"You can put your boots in the oven, but that don't make them biscuits."

Dallas deejay on Country Radio 105.3 FM

Protect
Yourself.

Protect
What
Can Protect
You.

Change naturally triggers our survival instincts. The more uneasy we are about how change might work to our disadvantage, the more consumed we become with defending our own best interests. The self-preservation motive crowds out our concern for the organization. "Looking out for old #1" takes priority over looking out for the customer.

As *individuals*, though, it's tough to protect ourselves from the upheavals caused by rapid change. We best defend our personal interests when we rely on collective effort. When we place our faith in the strength of numbers. When we join with coworkers to focus our attention and energy on shaping a customer oriented culture that can bring us safety and success.

The "everyone for himself/herself" attitude splinters the overall group effort without adding any safety for the individual. A culture of "me-ism" can only damage the organization's ability to protect its people *or* its clientele.

Since your job can never be secure in an insecure organization, it makes sense to invest your energy in protecting what can protect you. Think beyond the "me" issues. Focus instead on strengthening the organization so it can better serve. Rather than maneuver in an effort to protect yourself, do everything within your power to protect the customer. That builds a broad perimeter of defense that protects you best against the winds of change.

Ultimately, it is the customer who determines the fate of the organization.

"Enough about me. Now, let's talk about you. Tell me.
What do you think about me?"

Anonymous

~~Be~~
~~Loyal to~~
~~the~~
~~Culture.~~

Practice
Aloyalty.

Loyalty creates traitors in a rapidly changing world. It happens when the organization tries to change to fit the times, but the culture won't let it. Devotees of the old, established way of doing things wrap themselves in the company flag and resist change on the grounds of love and duty. This misguided loyalty cripples the organization's ability to adapt, and should be considered treason.

Over the years loyalty developed a good reputation. Long considered a virtue, loyalty got rewarded by service pins, automatic pay raises, and promotions. But today loyalty creates problems when people pledge allegiance to a culture that no longer should exist.

There is grave danger in being chained to outdated traditions. Or remaining faithful to worn out ways of doing things. Or honoring old values and beliefs that developed under very different circumstances.

You need to show some insensitivity to the organization's history in order to show the proper respect for its future. Be willing to break with the past. Rethink whether yesterday's heroes provide the right role models for people today. Celebrate achievements that make the organization more competitive, rather than sticking with old rites and rituals that reward people for the wrong things.

Being loyal to a culture that is suicidal is a dishonorable act. So ask yourself whether you can afford to worship the legacy of the old culture, or whether that will eventually kill the company. Defending the past cannot protect you from the future.

The absence of loyalty is not necessarily disloyalty. A culture of *aloyalty* is better than allegiance to outdated values, beliefs, and behaviors.

"When the age of the Vikings came to a close,
they must have sensed it. Probably,
they gathered together one evening, slapped each other
on the back and said, 'Hey, good job.'"

Jack Handey,
"Deep Thoughts" from Saturday Night Live

~~Believe in the Problems.~~

Have Faith
in the
Opportunities.

Change can be hard on hope. Problems, the natural offspring of change, fill our field of view. It's easy to focus on what's going wrong instead of searching out the possibilities and opportunities. Trouble just naturally draws attention. As soon as change starts throwing off sparks, people become preoccupied with all the headaches, aggravations, and fears. As they say in the newspaper business, "Bad news drives good news away."

Believing in the problems destroys our faith in the opportunities. We get discouraged. We lose our spirit. Our energy drains out through the cracks in our self-confidence. We are left disempowered and cynical in a culture of despair. It's a dangerous way to face the future.

We need to remember that opportunity often comes disguised as trouble. Rather than dwelling on the negatives, we need to attack problems with a can-do attitude. We do the best job of managing change when our mind set is relentlessly positive. Hope for tomorrow enables us to transcend the problems of today.

The way you think – the way you frame the situation – heavily influences your ability to deal with tough problems. Look beyond the bleakness of the moment and envision a brighter tomorrow. Think in terms of possibilities rather than limits. Search for openings that can lead to a better future.

Believe in the opportunities, and you help them appear. Keep the faith, and you contribute to a culture of optimism, hope, and expectancy.

"The perception of a problem is always relative.
Your headache feels terrific to the druggist."

Ramona E. F. Arnett,
President, Ramona Enterprises, Inc.

~~Blame~~
~~Others~~
~~for What You~~
~~Don't Like.~~

Take Personal
Responsibility
for Fixing
Things.

Today's accelerating rate of change is like a breeder reactor for problems. That's just the nature of progress. But as people watch one problem give birth to several more, they start searching for somebody to blame.

Badmouthing the bosses becomes a favorite pastime. Pointing fingers becomes the most popular form of exercise. The growing number of problems proves nothing, but is offered as hard evidence that the changes are wrong, or that the changes are being managed poorly. Of course, none of this has a crying chance of slowing down change or reducing the rate of problems. All it does is create a culture of blame.

Blaming comes easy. Complaining is a cakewalk. But the culture needs encouragers instead of complainers, fixers rather than blamers. Blaming uses up a lot of energy, but doesn't provide any real relief. Rather than lighten anyone's load, it just creates additional burdens.

Often blaming is employed as a defensive tactic. Pointing your finger at another person diverts attention from yourself. Accuse someone else of taking the wrong action, and that sort of gives you grounds for expecting them to fix things you don't like. Overall, blaming is a devious way of delegating responsibility. Rather than offer solid help to resolve problems, you put the monkey on someone else's back.

Identifying problems is fine. Just make sure you package topnotch solutions with your complaints. Come up with constructive ideas of your own instead of waiting for somebody else to fix things. Get busy doing what you can do instead of second-guessing somebody else's efforts. "Monday morning quarterbacking" gives some people the notion that they're contributing something meaningful, but really it's just a cheap, backhanded way of throwing more blame.

There are more than enough problems to go around, so take your share of the responsibility for fixing things. Push for a culture of personal accountability.

"Don't you wish you were me? I know I do."

Sign taped above elevator button
in office building

~~Act Like~~
~~an Adult.~~

Act Like a
Child.

Kids have a reputation for handling change a lot better than adults do. Children enjoy it and take it in stride. It's their nature to flex, to adapt. They readily bend, while grownups get set in their ways. Instead of resenting the difficulties of change the way older people do, kids just treat problems like another plaything.

Adults also bog down in routine and habit, but children won't settle for the boredom of "sameness." Kids insist on variety. Change is what keeps them from getting sleepy. They crave surprises and seek novel experiences. They love to learn. Youngsters are explorers at heart, and they're open to the unexpected. As a result, their life is a constant stream of "breakthroughs."

We need to approach the "new" the way we did when we were just a few years old. With curiosity, rather than worry. Willing to fumble our way along in the process of figuring out what works best. Quick to abandon any behavior in favor of more efficient new-found solutions. Relentless in our determination to learn. Consumed with our search for mastery, for continuous improvement, intent on finding a better way every day.

Adults try to cope with the challenge of change by "using their heads," trusting in logic, and drawing on experience. But as kids we followed our hearts as much as our heads. We trusted our creative instincts, our intuition, because our logical thinking skills had not yet developed. And since we had not been around long enough to learn much from the past, we did not get trapped by our old solutions. We did not get hung up on tradition.

As kids we did not dread the future, even though it was unpredictable, challenging, and full of problems we were unprepared for. We had fun with change. And we learned more, faster, than we ever have as adults.

We need to act like children again – create a culture that knows how to learn – and we can give the organization the keys to the kingdom.

"Why don't people get braver as they get older?"

Ashleigh Brilliant,

author

*"Predicting the future is easy.
It's trying to figure out what's going on
now that's hard."*

Fritz R. S. Dressler,

President, FRS Dressler Associates

ORDER FORM
Culture Shift

1-99 copies	_____ copies at 5.95 each
100-999 copies	_____ copies at 5.75 each
1,000-4,999 copies	_____ copies at 5.50 each
5,000-9,999 copies	_____ copies at 5.25 each
10,000 or more copies	_____ copies at 5.00 each

> To place orders, call toll free **800-992-5922**
> or drop your order in the mail using this order form.
> Orders may be faxed to **214-789-7900**.

Name _____

Job Title _____

Organization _____

Phone _____

Street Address _____ Zip _____

P.O. Box _____ Zip _____

City, State _____

Country _____

Purchase order number (if applicable) _____

Applicable sales tax, shipping and handling charges will be added. Prices subject to change.

Orders less than $100 require prepayment. $100 or more may be invoiced.

☐ Check Enclosed   ☐ Please Invoice

☐ **VISA**   ☐ **MasterCard**   ☐ **AMERICAN EXPRESS**

Account Number _____ Expiration Date _____

Signature _____

800-992-5922
Overnight or Second Day Deliveries Available via Federal Express or UPS.

PRITCHETT & ASSOCIATES, INC.
13155 Noel Road, Suite 1600, Dallas, Texas 75240
214-789-7999 • FAX 214-789-7900

95567

About the Author

Price Pritchett, Ph.D., is Chairman and CEO of Pritchett & Associates, Inc., a Dallas-based consulting firm known for its expertise in organizational change. He has worked with a broad range of companies going through major culture transitions related to mergers and acquisitions, downsizing, and restructuring. His firm's client list includes General Electric, IBM, General Signal, John Hancock Insurance, Ernst &Young, BellSouth, Manufacturer's Bank, and Gulf States Utilities.

Books by PRITCHETT & ASSOCIATES, INC.

* *Mergers: Growth in the Fast Lane*

* *A Survival Guide to the Stress of Organizational Change*

* *Firing Up Commitment During Organizational Change*

* *The Employee Handbook of New Work Habits for a Radically Changing World*

The Team Member Handbook for Teamwork

* *Culture Shift: The Employee Handbook for Changing Corporate Culture*

The Quantum Leap Strategy

you²: A High Velocity Formula for Multiplying Your Personal Effectiveness in Quantum Leaps

The Ethics of Excellence

The Employee Survival Guide to Mergers and Acquisitions

After the Merger: Managing the Shockwaves

Making Mergers Work: A Guide to Managing Mergers and Acquisitions

* *Business As UnUsual: The Handbook for Managing and Supervising Organizational Change*

* *The Employee Handbook for Organizational Change*

* *Team ReConstruction: Building A High Performance Work Group During Change*

* *High-Velocity Culture Change: A Handbook for Managers*

Service Excellence!

Smart Moves: A Crash Course on Merger Integration Management

* Training program also available. Please call 1-800-622-8989 for more information.

Call 214-789-7999 for information regarding international rights and foreign translations.

Achieve Maximum Impact!

Enhance *Culture Shift*'s powerful message with the 4-hour training program built around the hard-hitting message presented in the handbook. Help all your employees understand and apply the 16 specific guidelines for changing corporate culture.

Culture Shift Training Program

The blend of lecturettes, group and individual discovery exercises, and open discussions give participants a well-rounded grasp of the need for culture change. *Culture Shift* training drives the change program down to the grass roots level. Rank and file employees are assigned personal responsibility to help transform the culture. All participants are measured on their degree of resistance to change versus their willingness to facilitate a dramatic culture shift.

Use this quick-impact training program to:

- Focus employees on the three key traits of a change-adaptive culture: *Market Intimacy, Corporate Athleticism,* and *Innovativeness*
- Mobilize a company-wide effort to make the culture more competitive
- Confront each person with the role he or she is playing in culture change—design, default, or defiance
- Develop action plans that make each employee personally accountable for culture change

For more information call 1-800-622-8989

Management Consulting Services

Pritchett & Associates developed its in-depth expertise by working with Fortune 500 clients for over 20 years. The key to our success is an intimate understanding of organizations undergoing major change. We combine extensive, "hands-on" executive experience with an analytic, results-oriented approach to problem solving. Our consultants have the know-how to:

• Exploit instability rather than merely cope with change

• Assess your culture, organization, and management processes to develop high-impact change initiatives

• Move you from plans to accomplishments...to become an adaptive organization

• Apply leading edge change management expertise and merger integration services to your critical business challenges

Training Programs to Implement Change

Pritchett training programs build on the hard-hitting principles in our best-selling handbooks. These quick-impact, concentrated programs deliver a no-nonsense message on how to deal with today's rapidly changing business environment. Our training helps your organization:

• Accept—not resist—the predictable dynamics of change

• Underline why every employee must become a change agent

• Get people to take personal responsibility for making change work

• Protect—and even improve—operating efficiency and productivity

• Learn to communicate change effectively

• Keep employees focused on the "high-priority" issues—your business and your customers

• Recognize and capitalize on the opportunities created by change